D1754244

Francis Pe

Paul – My Hero

Francis Pe

Paul – My Hero

A children's book for adults too

A true story
on a Greek island in the Aegean Sea

AT Edition

© Text: Franz W. Peren, Unkel am Rhein, Germany, 2017

© Illustration: Daniel Maertins, Koenigswinter, Germany, 2017

© The map from Greece has been taken from
http://www.landkartenindex.de/kostenlos/?cat=139
Date of access: April 10, 2017

Translated from German into English by Alan Faulcon, Berlin, Germany, 2017

This book, including all contents, is copyright protected.
All rights reserved.

Reprinting or reproduction (including in part) in any format (print, photocopy or other method) and saving, processing, duplicating, and disseminating using electronic systems of any type, in whole or in part, is prohibited and punishable by law without the written consent of the author, Prof. Dr. Dr. Peren. All translation rights reserved.

Bibliographic information published by the Deutsche Nationalbibliothek
The Deutsche Nationalbibliothek lists this publication in the Deutsche Nationalbibliografie; detailed bibliographic data are available on the Internet at http://dnb.d-nb.de.

ISBN 978-3-89781-261-1

AT Edition Münster   2018

Auslieferung/Verlagskontakt:
Fresnostr. 2 D-48159 Münster   0 251-20 07 96 10
E-Mail: ate@at-edition.de   http://www.at-edition.de

For Jimmy. The tomcat next door.

It was summer. During holidays on a Greek island in the Aegean Sea. In the Aegean the sea has a particularly beautiful glitter. Like nowhere else in the world.

The island on which I spent my holidays is quite small. There are not very many cars and no traffic lights at all. Animals are not locked up in fenced properties. In general they are free to run around.

In many places where humans live there are also cats. On the Greek islands in any case, as their inhabitants love cats. Like most Greeks. Cats are allowed to live freely on the Greek islands. They create their own families, have friends and natural enemies. On the Greek islands cats live exactly like we humans live and want to live everywhere in the world: in freedom.

And so Cats on the Greek islands live their own natural life – with all of the advantages and disadvantages. The advantages of such a cat's life in its natural surroundings surely outweigh a cat's existence in an urban apartment or in a fenced garden, as is often the case in human societies.

The cats on the Greek islands also meet other cats every day and night. Good and bad animals of the same species. They eat within their own families. Play together with their friends. Fall in love. Start families. Have children together. This is completely different from most other areas in Europe. And for many months of the year it is warm and sunny on these islands. Cats love that too.

Like humans, there are also cats that are less lucky than others. One day such a cat appeared before the door to my terrace. It was a medium-sized, black tomcat. Without a thought I called him Paul.

Paul

Paul was not particularly large. But still, he was quite intimidating at first sight.

Even his head appeared to differ from what I was used to seeing among cats on the island. His head had the rectangular form of a panther's. All of the other cats here had pointed, V-shaped heads.

Paul's teeth were also unlike those of the other cats. The two eyeteeth at the top were much longer than those of the cats that I had previously encountered here on the island. Or maybe they just looked like that? Because Paul was a completely black tomcat, while all the other cats were white, light-gray and light brown or their fur was a combination of these bright colors in various nuances and mixtures. At times a cat was basically white, but here and there its fur had gray or light brown spots, while at other times it behaved in exactly the opposite manner.

It could certainly be frightening when a completely black tomcat suddenly appeared with unusually striking white teeth.

But the most unusual thing about Paul was his eyes. Paul squinted – squinted inward. Even if his eyes were a beautiful, bright greenish blue, a turquoise almost like the sea, his look was more frightening because of the squinting, particularly since his eyes did not immediately reveal whether Paul intended to be hostile or friendly towards you. And so, I too, was frightened at first.

Paul appeared to be irritated. He also shied away from me and my reluctance. But he was already used to that. Others – whether they were animals of the same species or humans – seemed to see something strange in him, an evil monster. Yet Paul was anything but wicked, as it turned out.

With "Uhhh ... uhhh...", a sound that I had never heard from a cat before, Paul now made it quite clear to me that he was very hungry. I quickly brought him something to eat out of the house.

Without even chewing he hastily gulped it down with just a few bites.

It was only now that I properly saw this little "monster", that of course was not a monster at all, but only looked different from all the other cats. His back was marked by intense fighting and physical disputes. His fur had been completely bitten out in one place. But now free from hair, it had completely healed in the meantime. Fresh pus oozed from a spot on his head and from an eye as well. When he ate he had to cough. He ate as though there were no tomorrow. When he was finally full after repeated feedings he disappeared. He did not clean himself. He did not rest. He just jumped over the next wall and disappearred.

I did not see him again that day, but I constantly had to think about this so-called "monster." How was he able to live? Survive? Is he a loner or did he live in a sheltered cat family? Does he have a permanent home? A permanent place to sleep? My questions were answered on the following day.

Paul came back the next day at about the same time. I had also hoped that it might turn out something like this. But this time he did not come alone, but instead in the company of a still very young cat.

I spontaneously called it Gregory, although at this point in time I was not sure whether Gregory was male or female.

Gregory

A short time later it was easy to see that Gregory was in fact a small tomcat. So I was able to stick with the name that I had spontaneously given him.

Gregory was still very young and very small – only a few weeks old. And he was completely undernourished. So his paws appeared very large in proportion to the rest of his small, very thin body. He looks more like a jumping mouse, I thought. The color of his fur was also similar to that of a mouse. Light brown with large white portions. His fur looked dull and ragged, which emphasized the fact that tiny Gregory was completely undernourished, probably already for quite some time now.

His ears that looked disproportionately large were also reminiscent of a jumping mouse and all in all he was also not much bigger than a large mouse anyway.

Both of his eyes watered. A festering secretion ran out of them. At irregular intervals he was forced to sneeze – usually several times in a row. Gregory was sick. He suffered from a cat's cold, an illness much worse and more dangerous than a cold among us humans, because cats often then remain ill for the rest of their life.

I imagined what it would be like to be sick every single day for your entire life. How you would live and feel if you could never breathe through your nose, and meals really had no taste – particularly since you also had to breathe through your mouth while eating – and you constantly felt run down and exhausted, with no real pleasure in life.

And all of the other cats around you play or enjoy a completely normal, everyday life, but you are hardly able to actually take part in normal everyday life. Not only for one or two weeks, but all the time – your entire life.

Paul & Gregory

Two thoughts shot through my head:

1. Little Gregory had to be helped. So what could I do as a human?

2. And why does Paul always bring him along? Especially because it was clear that Paul could not be Gregory's father.

Gregory's fur and the shape of his head were like that of all of the other cats here. But Paul had the angular head of a panther and was completely black. But Paul had brought him along, had led him to me.

Gregory pressed his small body closely against Paul. He was afraid: afraid of me, afraid of humans. But he trusted

Paul. Paul appeared to protect and guide him. He obviously seemed to care for Gregory. Why else would he bring him to me? How at all did Paul get this little guy over the high wall of natural stones that surround the house in which I live here on the island?

I set my questions aside for now. The first thing to do was to get them some food ...

The two of them shared the meal. When the little fellow was not able to reach the food he gently pressed Paul's large head to the side. But that was okay for Paul.

Aha, I thought, Paul is no monster, even if he might look like one. On the contrary, Paul takes care of little Gregory, who probably would have already starved without him. How would Gregory – who obviously no longer had a caring mother or father – have been able to survive alone? And at his age – only a few weeks old – in his undernourished and ill condition, Gregory surely would not have been able to care for himself alone.

But he apparently had Paul to take care of him. So there it was: Paul took care of Gregory, even though he was not his father. Of course Paul was also not his mother either. After all, Paul was a tomcat. And did not tomcats always leave it up to mothers, to the women, to take care of and raise small cats? That's what I had always seen up to now.

In the days that followed Paul and Gregory visited me two or three times a day in order for me to feed them.

Now and again I also fed them in the house in order to protect them against other cats when they were eating. Then I served the food on a plate to the two of them. Paul let the little guy have the first go. But that was not what Gregory wanted and so he stopped eating. So I divided up the meal onto two smaller plates. They then cleaned the one plate together, and after that they emptied the other one.

After a few days they were no longer in a hurry to get away from me after eating. First they both stretched themselves. Then they licked themselves clean. If Gregory had to sneeze, then Paul looked at him anxiously.

If Gregory had a habit of quickly hiding under my bed whenever we went into the house when we first became acquainted, after a few days of observing me very closely he then ran around inside the entire house and curiously sniffed on everything. At the same time he caused himself to jump if he happened to knock over an empty plastic bottle. Then Paul would give him a gentle punch with his paw and show him outside.

They came, ate and always left together; which confirmed my suspicion that Paul as a male took care of Gregory, who was unrelated to him. Paul was the one who protected and took care of Gregory.

So it was only with help from Paul that Gregory had a chance to survive and grow up to be an independent cat.

The Fat Cats

But my feedings also attracted other, particularly well-fed cats in the neighborhood. Although they were all doing quite well, they wanted to claim some of the food.

What should I do now? To escape with Gregory & Paul into the house without having other cats cleverly follow us was not always possible.

It was impossible to feed this entire bunch of cats. And besides, I really did not know all that much about cats; but I knew that there were hierarchies and natural priorities in a cat community.

And so the scene was dominated at the beginning by rather large, well-fed tomcats whom all of the other cats paid considerable respect. I also felt uneasy and cornered in their presence. Under no circumstances did I want to make these fat cats any fatter and stronger. And besides, I was afraid that Paul, who was not nearly as big and strong, could get into a fight or physical difficulties with these showoffs where he definitely would not have had a chance.

What about Gregory? Would he have been accepted by them running the neighborhood? Or would there have been the danger that these machos would fight and possibly even injure him too? I had no idea, but I was certain that it was up to me to make certain that these huge beasts disappeared before Paul and Gregory returned.

In order to do this I filled up several bottles with water and every time one of these snoopy and greedy despots showed up I poured a bottle of water over him. That helped. Cats, and even fat cats, do not like water.

The Mother Cat

I was still well-acquainted with a mother cat from the year before. She was a very nice cat. She also suffered from a cat's cold.

Her eyes watered sometimes more, and sometimes less. Otherwise she appeared to be quite strong and robust. She was very social and did not take food away from the other cats, even though she ate quite a lot and actually had to because, it was clear from her belly, she was pregnant again this summer. Like the year before. She already produced, or was even still producing, milk because two of her kittens who were nearly one year old now and looked to me like they were already grown up, strong and healthy, continued to be nursed by her at irregular intervals. This appeared to make both her and the little ones quite happy.

I immediately imagined that Gregory would be saved if he were given this mother's milk instead of her two already rather large offspring.

Unfortunately I was mistaken. When the mother cat met Gregory for the first time she sniffed at him and immediately knew that Gregory was not one of her family and not even a relative. And so she refused to help him, even as a mother, with mother's milk that was so important for Gregory. Not just now and today, but never.

I was shocked by her behavior. After all, the mother cat was a totally sweet animal, not at all aggressive or dominant like these fat cat show-offs. She was always very social and very caring when it came to her children. Even now, although her two boys were already young adults and had their own interests.

But she loved and cared only for her own family. She rejected strangers. Even if they, like little Gregory, were needy orphans of her own kind.

Paul was was also rejected by this fine feline. She hunched her back and made hissing sounds whenever they met. Paul did not seem to understand her refusal;

he then squinted at her in a calm, but disappointed fashion. Not a single time did he hiss back, even if he could have easily driven her away as the one who was clearly stronger.

He did not bother her even when I gave food to the mother cat. As an expecting mother once again she showed up often and asked for food. After all, she was pregnant and the new babies in her belly needed to grow and develop. Paul knew that. Without exception he always let her go first and waited calmly before he also gratefully accepted the food that I offered.

What a gentleman, I thought, particularly when eating meant survival both for him in his own weak physical condition and for his charge, Gregory.

The Cuddly Cat

One of the cat mother's two cat children was particularly noticeable. I called this practically fully grown tomcat the "cuddly cat" because this nearly one year old tomcat always wanted to cuddle at every chance.

He cuddled whenever there was an opportunity. He always attempted to be near to the other cats, but also to me as well as several other human guests at the holiday resort.

Love was the most important thing to him. Even eating was less important. If he was handed fresh food, then his hunger made him begin to eat quickly and hastily like all the rest of the cats as well. But if another cat came along, then he was friendly enough to leave the leftovers.

And that is how he also behaved toward Gregory, who was clearly much smaller and weaker than this nearly one year old, practically full-grown cat. But he did not cuddle with Gregory. He disappeared whenever Paul or Gregory showed up near him. Though thirsty for physical contact at any other time, he always made certain to steer clear of the two of them. For him they were strangers.

The Spotted Cat

The cuddly cat also had a sister from the same litter; a beautiful, female cat with a grayish-white spot of irregular size and position. She was attractive, and spotted in off-white.

Whenever there was something to eat she was able to articulate herself loudly and clearly, but quite charmingly. I was pleased to hear how she "spoke" with me. She understood us humans very well and had obviously noted that we communicate with one another through language.

If she was hungry, then she did not, like the other cats, rub her head against my leg or the back of my hand. Instead she made unmistakable sounds. Sometimes she sounded like this, sometimes like that, depending on what she needed at the time. I liked that. I also thought I understood her too.

The spotted cat was not only exceptionally attractive. Her behavior was also very elegant, because it was reserved. She never put herself in front of the other cats, but she always knew how to politely get what she wanted. Without a doubt, she was a lady.

I was all the more irritated when I heard for the first time that she gave little Gregory a rather nasty whack with her paw, and also used her claws in a less than ladylike manner at a moment when I was not looking.

At first I thought it was surely an exception and somehow justified. But over the course of time it was difficult not to see that this was deliberate behavior. Whenever Paul and I were not looking she gave Gregory a powerful, targeted slap with her paw, always right in front of her own family. In other words, the other cats who belonged here were supposed to see that she also did not like these newcomers, in this case little Gregory. From Paul she stayed away.

The Glutton

Another small tomcat, about half a year old – and who I called the "glutton" – always pushed himself into the front row whenever there was something to eat.

If I scattered food out in front of him, then his eyes were already fixed on the food of the other cats. He often pushed himself into the meals of other cats and drove them away from their food. After hastily devouring the food of the other cats, he then turned his attention to the food that was really meant for him.

How he was able to dominate like this as the clearly smallest cat – except for Gregory – was a mystery to me. Particularly because all of the other cats were much larger and stronger than him. What a greedy egotist, I thought. He was already quite round and plump, but he could never get enough. He pushed his way into every feeding opportunity, but never shared anything.

It was easy for him to chase away little Gregory. The glutton always pounced on his food first before Gregory could even begin with his meal. And then the glutton would eat up every bit of it. In the meantime Gregory sat directly in front of him and sadly watched as the glutton gobbled down his entire plate. Nothing, not even the smallest crumb, was left for Gregory.

Were it not for Paul, who usually sized up the situation very quickly and then chased the aggressor away from Gregory's food, the glutton would have always eaten everything by himself: Gregory's portion, that of the other cats and finally his own.

Just like us humans, I thought. There are egotists among us as well who only think about themselves and often rob their fellow human beings as well as animals and plants of their habitat and existence.

How fortunate for Gregory that he had Paul as his friend and protector. Without Paul he would have starved in competition with the larger and stronger cats. Despite the abundance of food for everyone, they would have eaten his portion as well. Thank goodness there was Paul.

The Beauty

There was one cat that was particularly beautiful and graceful. I had never seen such a beautiful cat before.

She was apparently aware of the impression she made on others. She was not only unusually attractive. But the way she looked and moved was enchanting. I was always happy to see her. And feeding her was a particular joy. She did not like to eat from the ground at all. She wanted to have her food on a plate. No problem. I thought that was also very special and elegant.

One night when I went outside again – day was already dawning – I found this cat also in my small garden behind the house. But this time she did not appear to be lovely and striking at all. Her eyes were filled with hate. Her look and her deep dislike were aimed at little Gregory who she had pounced on with her entire, full-grown body and attacked with firm blows and open claws. As I promptly chased off the beauty I noticed that she had bitten out a piece of Gregory's ear.

Unfortunately this malicious, deceitful behavior did not remain an exception, so whenever she appeared again I used water to run her out of my garden, just like the shameless fat cats before her.

Actually I should have questioned the true character of this exceptionally attractive beauty much earlier because it was clear that she did not like Paul from the very beginning.

Unfortunately though, that is how we humans often are. We allow ourselves to be enticed and taken in by outward appearances. Beauty fascinates us. On the other hand, we avoid others who do not fit our image of what is beautiful or at least normal.

I was charmed by the beautiful cat, while I had been frightened of Paul. Unlike animals, we humans rely all too much on our eyes. We believe and trust what we see. But compared with many animals our eyes are inferior in quality – even if we wear glasses.

But what other choice do we have as humans than to rely on what we see? After all, in contrast to Paul and other animals we also do not have a particularly good sense of smell. And compared with animals in general, our sense of touch is not particularly well developed. Anyhow, now I was ashamed of being so superficial and so stupid that I was able to be deceived by the beauty of this cat.

Humans

Of course I did not live alone at this holiday facility. Other people also spend their holidays here. Unfortunately, I only understood some of them because we humans – in contrast to cats – do not all speak the same language. But I did understand their sounds gestures.

These included shooing away the cats. Many of the humans did not like cats. "Shoo ... shoo ..." could then be heard. At the same time they waved with their hands as though they were in need of help.

The cats were of course already familiar with this human behavior. They understood that they were not welcome, and so they disappeared. Some of the particularly hungry cats still attempted to beg for food here or elsewhere – but usually without success.

I did not understand people who behaved in this way. After all, the people on vacation here were all very wealthy.

They boarded airplanes that brought them here. They lived in hotels. They even rented cars or motorcycles while on holidays. I heard them laugh and celebrate on their terraces or balconies almost every evening. They ate and drank well and in abundance. But they chased away the cats, our animal friends with whom we were able to share our lives at the same time and at the same place, whenever they asked for a daily meal.

Farewell

There came the day that never fails to come: the day of parting. My vacation had come to an end. Now I had to take leave of Paul and Gregory.

Gregory was now nearly twice as large as he was on the day when he stood in front of my door for the first time. Unfortunately he was not completely rid of his cat's cold, but now his coat was shiny and his eyes had stopped watering – and now he jumped and ran around brimming over with life.

Unfortunately, except for Paul, only one of the cats that belonged to the holiday facility had made friends with him. In fact it was the glutton who enjoyed playing with him now. I often saw them playing together or climbing up the trees.

All of the other cats continued to avoid my dear new friends Paul and Gregory.

The mother cat had only sniffed at Gregory once upon their first meeting and then obviously decided to avoid Paul and Gregory for good.

The cuddly cat was too much of a coward to do anything that the group did not approve. He was a nice fellow without a doubt. He offered love to the cats that he knew – instead of being a macho like the fat cats that ruled the neighborhood. But he remained weak outside of his own community. He wanted to be loved by the cats in his family and the usual neighbors – and so he was. But like his mother and sister, the spotted one, he scorned foreigners. Gregory and Paul never had a chance.

The beauty turned out to be sneaky and dishonest. Once she even bit off a piece of little Gregory's ear.

So Paul and Gregory basically remained alone during my holidays, for the most part separated from the community of the traditional cats, even if the glutton played with Gregory more frequently and the two enjoyed tussling with one another.

Paul had become strong. His dark coat was shiny and his bluish green, almost turquoise-colored eyes were particularly beautiful and exotic as a contrast to his now so shiny black fur.

The fact that he squinted no longer mattered.

Paul remained faithful to his own voluntary duty to look after Gregory. He intervened immediately if any of the other cats tried to harass Gregory. Paul looked out for him day and night.

Paul devoted his full time and attention to Gregory, who was a complete stranger. He was not his father, nor was he related to him. He was simply there for Gregory. For as long as Gregory would need him.

Paul not only protected and fed Gregory, he also gave the little guy love and security. After all, like humans, cats need more than just meals to be happy – they need affection and attention as well.

Perhaps Paul would have preferred to take care of his own affairs. Instead he sacrificed his very own interests and pleasures, those of an adult and impresssive tomcat.

The well-being and survival of his friend and charge Gregory were worth more to him. I decided that Paul is a hero for me. Even if I did not know exactly what a hero was or how a hero was supposed to be. A hero is surely someone who puts his own life and well-being in the service of someone else. And that is exactly what Paul did.

The other cats also recognized that Paul was a good guy and not a monster. They still did not let Paul and Gregory take part in their lives with their families; but now they treated Paul with approval and respect. Even the fat cats let the two of them move around in their district. They stopped attacking Paul and Gregory. My plastic bottles filled with water were no longer needed.

It was not only my food that made Paul into an impressive and respected tomcat. He became strong and handsome above all on his own. Not only had he fought and asked for food for himself as all the other cats had done. He did so also for Gregory. His sharing, his active responsibility for someone else's abandoned kitten made him into what he is today.

One Last Look

On my last day of vacation I could hardly take my eyes off the two of them. Paul and Gregory had been such a great pleasure. They had given me so much.

Paul taught me that one had to accept and make strangers a part of one's own life in order to be happy. Gregory had also been a stranger to Paul. Yet Paul did not simply abandon him and leave him to take care of himself. Like all of the other cats would have done. He took care of him, and in the end he found his own happiness by doing so.

It was already clear to Paul and Gregory that I was about to leave them. My packed suitcase, the change of clothes, and my unusual behavior – they were already familiar with this from previous holiday guests. As I carried my suitcase out of the house Gregory looked at me rather sadly with his eyes of different colors and ears that no longer appeared quite so large. I also found it difficult to say farewell to my two new friends that I had become so fond of.

In the morning when the sun came up and the first dogs started to bark and the roosters began to crow on the island, Paul and Gregory had already been waiting in front of my house until I opened the door and gave them something to eat.

Several of the holidays guests had already complained about my "fussing" around with these cats. But the owners of the holiday facility let me do as I pleased – because the Greeks love cats, particularly on the Aegean Islands.

Here is where the three of us, Paul, Gregory and I, had only just become acquainted with each other a few weeks ago and had spent a wonderful time with one another.

Ever since that day when Paul brought Gregory along the two of them often stood in front of my house and waited. And I waited for them as well. Early in the morning I would lie in bed and begin to listen out for the two of them. Now and then I noticed when Paul jumped onto the table in front of my window and listened into my bedroom through the closed shutters. But both cats waited calmly and patiently until I appeared in the door.

It was a particularly pleasant feeling whenever Paul first welcomed me by pressing his head against the back of my hand.

Although Gregory kept his distance during the first few days, he dared to come closer with each passing day. After about a good week he began to imitate Paul. Then he too pressed his small head against me in the morning as his way of saying good morning.

Later on, in the early afternoon, I usually laid down in the shade of a tree in order to get a little sleep. Paul and Gregory would then often lay down under a bush not far away from me and slept as well. Little Gregory usually rested right on top of Paul, where he clearly was most comfortable.

In the last week of my holidays Gregory often climbed on top of me as well whenever I was asleep outdoors. The little fellow would then lie down on my chest and purr loudly and without stop. Finally, he also fell asleep. Then I hardly dared to get up because I noticed that Gregory now liked being close to me. Our friendship and mutual trust was good for him. After all, as we already know from Paul, cats need more than just food to be happy – they need love and attention.

All of these wonderful moments which we three shared with one another during the three weeks that Paul and Gregory had devoted to me, all of that would be over today. As I stood there now with my packed suitcase, having to actually say goodbye to Paul and Gregory – well, how was I to just turn around and simply walk away from the two of them?

At that moment Paul discovered a beetle on the ground and showed it to Gregory. Gregory immediately jumped over to the beetle full of curiosity and delight, sniffed it and tried to catch his first natural prey with paws that were certainly quite large for a beetle.

Paul also acted as if he was completely fascinated by this tiny little beetle, cleverly turning his questioning eyes away from me. Where was he supposed to get food in the future; and Gregory for that matter? What would become of our friendship? Would we three ever see each other again?

Paul, whom I was afraid of at first because he gave me the impression of being a little "monster", was even helping me now. He realized how difficult it was for me to leave, but that the inescapable time had come to depart.

And so Paul "discovered" the beetle. In doing so he not only drew their attention away from this awkward scene of departure. Paul also gave me – the human being – the opportunity to leave the two of them "unnoticed." What a guy, what a hero – this little "monster", I quietly chuckled.

Paul and Gregory had already stopped chasing the beetle as I turned around at the end of the house wall to look at the two of them for one last moment before I finally disappeared around the corner. The beetle had cleverly escaped between the stones and leaves. Tomorrow they would come across another beetle or something else new.

After all, the island was full of fascinating things to discover and interesting opportunities. And full of happiness. Not only for cats.

Epilogue

This table is based on a true story.

This is Paul

67

This is Gregory

...and this is Jimmy, a true friend to whom this book is dedicated.

The End